For :-

Joseph Rowe

From :-

Rosalie

Grandfathers Are Special

GRANDFATHERS ARE SPECIAL

Warmhearted Writings
By and About Grandpas

• • •

Edited by Aileene Herrbach Neighbors
Illustrated by Wendie Collins

Hallmark Editions

The publisher wishes to thank those who have given their kind permission to reprint material included in this book. Every effort has been made to give proper acknowledgments. Any omissions or errors are deeply regretted, and the publisher, upon notification, will be pleased to make necessary corrections in subsequent editions.

ACKNOWLEDGMENTS: "My Favorite Sport" from *The Laugh's on Me* by Bennett Cerf. Copyright © 1959 by Bennett Cerf. Reprinted by permission of the publisher, Doubleday & Co., Inc. "The Expectant Grandfather's Guidebook" by Floyd Miller. © 1968 by Harvest Years Publishing Co. "The New Joys in His Life" from "Meet the New Sam Levenson — Grandfather" by Helen Alpert from the May, 1975, issue of *Retirement Living*. Copyright © 1975 by Harvest Years Publishing Co. Reprinted by permission. "Let's Have a Family Reunion" by Frank Howard Richardson. Copyright © 1964 by Frank Howard Richardson. From the book *Grandparents and Their Families*. Reprinted with permission of David McKay Co., Inc. "Rent a Grandpa — 10¢" from "Grandparents" by Sharon Curtin from the December 2, 1973, *New York Times Magazine*. © 1973 by The New York Times Company. Reprinted by permission. Excerpt "Was there ever…" by Joe E. Wells from the October 11, 1953, *New York Times Magazine*. © 1953 by The New York Times Company. Reprinted by permission. "A Very Special Relationship" from "Grandparents Are to Love" by Rita M. Fuerst reprinted by permission from the August, 1967, issue of *Parents' Magazine*, New York, U.S.A. Copyright © 1967 by Parents' Magazine Enterprises. "Is There a Grandpa in the House?" by Rita Kramer reprinted by permission from Volume XLIX, No. 5 issue of *Parents' Magazine*, New York, U.S.A. Copyright © 1974 by Parents' Magazine Enterprises. Excerpt from the writings of George Bernard Shaw reprinted by permission of The Society of Authors on behalf of the Bernard Shaw Estate. "Play Ball!" from "Grandfather and the Racquet-tailed Drongo" by Jonathan Rhoades from *Sports Illustrated*, February 28, 1966. © Time Inc. 1966. Reprinted by permission of the author and the author's agents, Scott Meredith Literary Agency, Inc., 845 Third Avenue, New York, New York 10022. "Garland for Grandfather" by Gladys McKee from *Good Housekeeping*. © Hearst Corporation. Reprinted by permission. "December Poem for Grandfather" by Gladys McKee from *The Saturday Evening Post*. © Curtis Publishing Company. Reprinted by permission.

© 1977, Hallmark Cards, Inc., Kansas City, Missouri. Printed in the United States of America. Standard Book Number: 87529-503-7.

Grandfathers
Are Special

IS THERE A
GRANDPA IN THE HOUSE?

Rita Kramer, writer and coauthor with Dr. Lee Salk of How to Raise a Human Being, *describes grandpa and the vital role he (and grandma, too) can play in his grandchildren's lives.*

Janos Koscka is a retired cabinetmaker who learned his craft as a youth in his native Hungary. Peter, his nine-year-old grandson, is learning wood-turning from him on the lathe in the basement of the Koscka's two-family house on the west side of Chicago.

In San Francisco's Chinatown, ten-year-old Kim Soong stacks rice cakes, while his sister Lin, eight, wraps them in plastic for the customers in their grandfather's teashop-bakery.

Tom Mundy is spending his 60th birthday with his seven-year-old grandson, Dennis. They are sitting in comfortable silence in a rowboat in the middle of a Vermont lake, waiting patiently for the fish to bite.

These three grandfathers are sharing something precious — and unfortunately rare these days — with their grandchildren, to the benefit of both generations. Passing on skills, transmitting family history, giving the young their first chance to be of real help, or just being there in undemanding companionship — these are some of the roles grandparents have played since history began. Doing so has given a fuller meaning, an extra dimension, to the lives of young people and older ones, too. In fact, it is what makes a family a family....

A child who has heard his grandparents' stories of the old country, or "the time when your mother was a little girl," knows who he is because he knows where he comes from and which experiences led to his being alive, here and now. He learns something about life that only those who have lived many years can teach, though they often provide these lessons without knowing that they're doing so....

Today, more than ever, young children need personal touchstones to the past. These are, in fact, their passports to the future. That is why children who do grow up spending considerable time with their grandparents are fortunate indeed.

A third-grader I know told me, "My grandmother makes bread every week. It doesn't

have paper around it; it just comes in itself."
A ten-year-old riding in the same station wagon
with us added, "My grandpa used to work in
rodeos with real cowboys. That was out west.
Come over to our house and he'll tell you
about it." …

All the generations of a family gain something from involvement with each other. The
oldest realize that their life still has meaning,
the youngest learn more about what men and
women are like, and discover more options
to choose from in developing their own style.
They gain valuable experiences in learning
to get along with others, and in being loved
and loving in return. The in-between genera-
tion — the young parents — gain emotional
support and the practical help of an extra
pair of hands.

WHAT IS A GRANDFATHER?

A grandfather has a special talent...
He always knows just what to do
To make his grandchildren happy
And to show that he loves them, too.
He has his own favorite armchair
For reading or taking a nap
Or telling his wonderful stories
To children who sit on his lap.
At the family get-togethers,
He's the first person to look for.
He can entertain small children for hours,
And they always keep asking for more.
You can tell when a grandfather is teasing
By the twinkle that shines in his eyes.
He's an expert at settling problems,
For he's loving and patient and wise.
His grandchildren always admire him,
Even when they are grown;
They always feel proud and happy
To claim Grandfather as their own!

Kay Andrew

COMING TO AMERICA

I was twelve years old before I saw my grandfather. Mama and Papa and I lived in a small
village in Hungary, but my grandfather had
gone to the United States about a year before I was born. Ever since I can remember,
my parents told me that one day we would
move to a wonderful place called "America" —
the country where Grandfather lived. He
was working hard to send us the fare so we
could all be together. To me, Grandfather
seemed more like a saint than an ordinary
person. While I was growing up, he was like
the prince I heard about in fairy tales — the
wonderful prince who always made everyone
happy ever after.

But one day, the fairy tale became very
real. We were traveling to America at last and
I was going to meet *him* — Grandfather. I was
too frightened of that meeting to even feel
sad about leaving or excited about the long
trip. All I can recall about the boat ride is
that I kept wondering, "Will he like me? Will
he be disappointed in me? Will he be glad I
am coming to live with him?"

When the ship finally docked, and we walked down the long ramp to shore, I pressed very close to my mother. There were so many people in this strange place — all shouting and waving. Then, all of a sudden, I felt myself being lifted up and hugged so tightly I could hardly breathe.

"Perileh! Mine Perileh!" a masculine voice cried through tears and smiles. And then I knew that the big man with the long red beard who was holding me in his arms was my own grandpa. And it was me — his Pearl — that he was happiest to see.

Pearl Weiss

. . .

Was there ever a grandparent, bushed after a day of minding noisy youngsters, who hasn't felt the Lord knew what He was doing when He gave little children to young people?

Joe E. Wells

A NEW HOME FOR HEIDI

In the famous children's story Heidi *by Johanna Spyri, the charming little girl is entrusted to the care of her beloved grandfather. Their first evening together in the little Alpine cottage is a moving experience for both of them.*

The time passed happily on till evening. Then the wind began to roar louder than ever through the old fir trees; Heidi listened with delight to the sound, and it filled her heart so full of gladness that she skipped and danced round the old trees, as if some unheard of joy had come to her. The grandfather stood and watched her from the shed.

Suddenly a shrill whistle was heard. Heidi paused in her dancing, and the grandfather came out. Down from the heights above the goats came springing one after another, with Peter in their midst. Heidi sprang forward with a cry of joy and rushed among the flock, greeting first one and then another of her old friends of the morning. As they neared the hut the goats stood still, and then two of their number, two beautiful slender animals, one white and one brown, ran forward to where the grandfather was standing and began licking his hands, for he was holding a little salt which he always had ready for his goats on their return home. Peter disappeared with the remainder of his flock. Heidi tenderly stroked the two goats in turn, running first to one side of them and then the other, and jumping about in her glee at the pretty little animals. "Are they ours, grandfather? Are they both ours? Are you going to put them in the shed? Will they always stay with us?"

Heidi's questions came tumbling out one after the other, so that her grandfather had only time to answer each of them with "yes, yes." When the goats had finished licking up the salt her grandfather told her to go and fetch her bowl and the bread.

Heidi obeyed and was soon back again. The grandfather milked the white goat and filled her basin, and then breaking off a piece of bread, "Now eat your supper," he said, "and then go up to bed. Cousin Dete left another little bundle for you with a nightgown and other small things in it, which you will find at the bottom of the cupboard if you want them. I must go and shut up the goats, so be off and sleep well."

"Good-night, grandfather! good-night. What are their names, grandfather, what are their names?" she called out as she ran after his retreating figure and the goats.

"The white one is named Little Swan, and the brown one Little Bear," he answered.

"Good-night Little Swan, good-night, Little Bear!" she called again at the top of her voice, for they were already inside the shed. Then she sat down on the seat and began to eat and drink, but the wind was so strong that it almost blew her away; so she made haste and finished her supper and then went indoors and climbed up to her bed, where she was soon lying as sweetly and soundly asleep as any young princess on her couch of silk.

Not long after, and while it was still twilight, the grandfather also went to bed, for he was up every morning at sunrise, and the sun came climbing up over the mountains at a very early hour during these summer months. The wind grew so tempestuous during the night, and blew in such gusts against the walls, that the hut trembled and the old beams groaned and creaked. It came howling and wailing down the chimney like voices of those in pain, and it raged with such fury among the old fir trees that here and there a branch was snapped and fell. In the middle of the night the old man got up. "The child will be frightened," he murmured half aloud. He mounted the ladder and went and stood by the child's bed.

Outside the moon was struggling with the dark, fast-driving clouds, which at one moment left it clear and shining, and the next swept over it, and all again was dark. Just now the moonlight was falling through the round window straight on to Heidi's bed. She lay under the heavy coverlid, her cheeks rosy with sleep, her head peacefully resting on her little round arm, and with a happy expression on her baby face as if dreaming of something pleasant. The old man stood looking down on the sleeping child until the moon again disappeared behind the clouds and he could see no more, then he went back to bed.

PLAY BALL!

Pursuing a hobby after retirement is generally good advice. Here, sports writer Jonathan Rhoades describes his retired grandfather's enthusiastic but brief attempt at managing a boys baseball team.

Three afternoons a week he had them working out, kids 6 to 10 years old, practicing sign-stealing and catcher's interference and learning how to bunt against a doctored infield. Mother always said that Grandfather's rapport with the little kids came from the fact that "he's 75 going on 9!" Personally, I felt it was because Grandfather talked to the boys the way a slightly older boy would talk, minus all the patronizing baloney we would get from other adults. "Look, Alberti," Grandfather would say to a lazy shortstop, "if you don't want to move your fanny why don't you just drag it off the field?" When a first baseman would circle and circle under a pop-up and then watch it bounce 10 feet behind him, Grandfather would say, "That was very nicely done, Mr. Nijinsky. Now what's your next number, the minuet?"

You might think that a manager with a sarcastic tongue like Grandfather's would be disliked by some of his players, but not so. Grandfather gave out cookies and pop, which he took from my mother's pantry. Also, the boys learned words and expressions from Grandfather that they would not normally have picked up till they took woodshop in the seventh grade under Mr. MacPherson. And anyway, Grandfather's vicious vocabulary came in handy at game time. The umpire would call, "Ball one!" on our pitcher, and Grandfather's foghorn voice would be heard all over the neighborhood calling out a reference to the ump's disgusting dietary habits. "Ball two!" the ump would say, and Grandfather would accuse him of performing bizarre physical feats. On "Ball three!" Grandfather would cup his hands to his mouth and make a public charge that there was a canine in the ump's family tree. After this how many umps do you think would call a ball four on our pitchers?

The whole trouble was that Grandfather got himself too wrought up, too personally involved. He would take the losses home with him, and late at night we would hear him crying out from his attic room in his sleep: "The infield fly rule? The *infield fly rule?* You have the guts to call the infield fly rule on a little kid? Why, you — —!" The next morning he would come to breakfast all red-eyed and pasty-faced, and he would sit there and stare at his food and answer in one-syllable words that made it plain that he didn't want to talk. After two or three seasons of this the family doctor told Grandfather that he would have to hang up his spikes. The old man took it hard; he stayed in his room for a couple of weeks, just coming out for meals and baths. He perked up a little at the news that his team had lost four straight games in his absence, but a two-game winning streak sent him down in the dumps again. This was when the doctor told him to look for outside interests, anything but managing an athletic team.

A BIRTHDAY LETTER FOR GRANDPA

Remember, Grandpa?
When Daddy worked late at the office,
Mom was at the P.T.A.,
Remember the chess and the checkers
And all the games we would play?
Remember the books you read me,
The ball games on T.V.,
Remember the stories about the farm
And when you were little like me?
Remember our secret parties
With pretzels and ice cream and cake,
We laughed a lot and were silly
And the funniest faces we'd make.
And because you made me
Happy then,
Just as you do today,
I love you and remember you
And every night I say:
"GOD BLESS my GRANDPA!"

Violet Bigelow Rourke

A VERY SPECIAL RELATIONSHIP

Scott Carpenter, the second American astronaut to orbit the earth, speaks glowingly of his childhood relationship with his grandfather. Together they explored the wild Colorado country on the outskirts of the town where young Scott learned from his grandfather about living in the woods, tying knots, and splicing rope.

To this day, the astronaut considers his grandfather a major influence in his life. He gave the boy his first job — peddling newspapers — and a sense of responsibility. He passed on to him a set of values and the benefit of a lifetime's experiences. And young Scott Carpenter revered his grandfather "as no boy ever respected another man."

Rita M. Fuerst

A MATTER OF SIZE

It's hard to imagine that fathers
Were ever little boys,
Playing ball and flying kites
And making lots of noise.

So once we asked Grandfather
If he remembered when
Dad was just a little boy
And what he was like back then.

Gramps chuckled a little and murmured,
"Well, now, I ought to say
He was quiet and well-mannered,
Perfect in every way.

"But, truth was, he was full of mischief —
Put frogs in the cookie jar,
Did outlandish tricks on fences,
Teased little girls and — chewed tar."

And we never told Dad what Grandfather said,
But we were so glad to realize
Being perfect must be a grown-up thing,
Mainly a matter of size.

R. Hurley

A GRANDFATHER'S SPECIAL LOVE

What could be more wonderful
Than a grandfather's special love —
He always seems to know the things
That we are fondest of,
He's always ready with a smile
Or a loving word of praise,
His laughter always brightens up
The cloudiest of days,
He has an understanding heart
That encourages and cheers,
The love he gives so freely
Grows deeper with the years,
His wisdom and devotion
Are blessings from above —
Nothing could be more wonderful
Than a grandfather's special love.

Mary Dawson Hughes

GRANDFATHER
BLOWING THE SHOFAR

The Jewish New Year was always a time of great excitement for me as a child. It was a happy time. We ate apples with honey on them, sent "Shanah Tovahs," or greetings, to our friends and prayed to God for a good year. But what I remember most of all about the holiday was my grandfather blowing the Shofar – the ram's horn – in the synagogue. Now it's really hard to get any sound at all out of a Shofar. I know because I tried year after year, and all I'd ever get was a thin little whistle. But not grandfather. When he blew the Shofar, its beautiful notes could be heard in every corner of the building, summoning people to pray. Then the congregation would smile and nod their approval as they chanted the traditional prayers and psalms with full hearts.

Sitting there, listening, I used to believe that God himself was standing next to grandfather, coaching him along. Come to think of it, maybe He was.

Blanche Weiss Hacker

DECEMBER POEM FOR GRANDFATHER

This is the time of year that he will go,
Secretly smiling at the depth of snow,

And hitch his horse up in the early light
When it is almost day and almost night.

Before the children waken he will be
Back to the barn. His trip a mystery

Not to be told until on Christmas day
The scent of cedar has its fragrant way

And fills the house till we are almost mad
With cedar scent and holly, being glad.

This is the time of year I think of him
And trace among the trees, though it is dim

His dear, familiar form that picks and chooses
All of the Christmas trees that Santa uses.

Gladys McKee

LET'S HAVE A FAMILY REUNION

Sometimes family get-togethers turn into free-for-alls. Frank Howard Richardson, a doctor, tells in his book Grandparents and Their Families *how one grandpa saved the vacation for all.*

The years galloped by for one couple, and that day arrived when their dream was to be realized in a real family reunion. Yes, all their grandchildren were to be there together. There would be a gang of them, ranging in age from two to fifteen. They would be almost like strangers to one another, but they would have Grandma and Grandpa in common. That would be the tie that would bind.

The first day, all went well. All were on their best behavior. A certain strangeness permeated the group. But that lasted for only one day. Then the fur began to fly. Clothes were dropped on the floor, dishes were smashed, doors were banged, and pandemonium prevailed. Each wanted to do what *he* wanted, irrespective of what anyone else wanted to do.

Grandpa, who was experienced in directing gangs of men, put on his thinking cap. He knew that something had to be done. This could not be allowed to keep on. The parents were helpless — but the grandparents were not! The children were always on their side, always. And, after all, they were the host and hostess, and the grandchildren were guests in their home.

So when night came, Grandpa called all the children to a meeting in the big living room. Parents were invited to sit on the sidelines and observe, but not to take part in the proceedings. It was to be a very formal affair. For a club was to be formed, and every grandchild could participate.

Grandpa was the chairman, and the spokesman. He was well dressed, and his manner was very serious, as if this were a courtroom. He announced to the assembled group that a club was to be formed, but one that was different from any other club. Most clubs have a rule that you have to pay dues. But in this club, the sponsor would pay the members to join! …Each one in the senior group would get 50 cents a week, the cubs would get 10 cents.

That *really* made them sit up and listen! And they shouted approval.

"But of course there will be rules," Grandpa added. "And if you break one of the rules, 2 cents will be deducted for every rule that is broken. But you yourselves are going to make the rules. Is that fair?" There was a unanimous chorus of yeses. And so the club was formed — the 3-C Club for Conduct, Consideration, and Courtesy.

In addition to the Senior Charter Members and Cub Charter Members, who were paid to belong, there was to be a Board of Judges (adults). The club was to meet every Saturday night, at which time members would be paid, and when there would be a full discussion of the conduct of each member during the week.

The following rules, suggested by the Board of Judges, were to be passed on by the charter members:

    (1) Put everything back in its place, where it belongs

    (2) Pick up anything thrown on the floor

    (3) Have something interesting to talk about at each meal

(4) Eat or drink all snacks in the yard, not on the porch or in the living room

(5) Wash all dishes *at once,* don't pile them in the sink

(6) No quarreling or raised voices at meals

(7) No fighting over who performed assigned duties

(8) No failing to perform a duty

(9) Judges to assign a duty to each member — changes could be made in these duties, if each change was approved by the Board of Judges

(10) If a diary was kept, with a full-page entry for each day, 25 cents would be given as a bonus

When the rules were all read and accepted, one boy called out, "Gee, this sounds to me like Alcatraz." (He proved to be one of the best in observing the rules himself and in leading others to observe them.)

How did all this work out? The whole attitude and conduct of everyone changed in a way that was almost too good to be true, and the parents looked on in wonder. They were

in charge when short trips were taken for
swimming or for horseback riding by smaller
groups; but at mealtimes, and in the evening,
when all returned to the big house, Grandpa
ruled supreme.

· · ·

GARLAND FOR GRANDFATHER

His speech was starred with adages,
He kept them just as handy
As nickels in his pockets
For sticks of striped candy;
"No news is good news," short, discreet,
Made the longest silence sweet,
"A stitch in time," "too many cooks...,"
I find them in old copy books
The heart kept in some secret place
Against whatever dark hours pace
The pulse of courage. He must know
How often now the mind must go
To find swift solace and to ponder...
"Absence makes the heart grow fonder."

Gladys McKee

GRANDPA'S TOOL SHED

Grandpa's tool shed is a special place,
Full of mystery and delight,
Where little kids can come and watch
While Grandpa builds a kite.

Each day before the sunset,
Grandpa is always there,
The sound of his saw and hammer
Filling the evening air.

Grandpa can fix anything
And make it look brand new —
He fixes toy cars and airplanes,
Trucks and trailers, too.

There are many happy moments
Pleasant to recall,
But Grandpa in his tool shed
Is the nicest one of all.

Shifra Stein

MY FAVORITE SPORT

I think you'll like this anecdote told to me by Warren Wire, of Los Angeles. "Last Christmas," he writes, "my daughter and son-in-law and their six-year-old Steven were among our guests. After dinner, we watched a football game on television, and that led to a general discussion of sports.

"One said he liked prize fights best; another golf; a third baseball. Somebody finally asked young Steven what kind of sport he liked best. He looked in turn at everybody in the room, then came over and threw his arms around me, and said, 'MY GRAN'PA.'"

Bennett Cerf

• • •

Life is no brief candle to me. It is a sort of splendid torch which I have got hold of for the moment, and I want to make it burn as brightly as possible before handing it on to future generations.

George Bernard Shaw

RENT A GRANDPA — 10¢

One summer, I picked up Saturday movie money by renting my grandfather to my friends. For a dime, they could watch him whittle a chain and a whistle from one piece of birchwood and, as a bonus, he would sometimes talk as he whittled. During those lazy hot afternoons he told stories of Indians and blizzards and how barbed wire ruined the wilderness; he made us hear wolves howl and feel the ground shake as the buffalo stampeded. Week after week, Granddad gave my friends and me the gift of his past. He made the way our elders had lived intelligible and real. It was much more entertaining and exciting than the movies I saw with the money I collected.

Sharon Curtin

THE EXPECTANT GRANDFATHER'S GUIDEBOOK

Floyd Miller, a veteran grandfather of three months, offers a few simple rules for patriarchs, one of which is being very patient with Grandma.

1. FACE UP TO THE FACTS OF LIFE.

When my son and daughter-in-law announced the approaching event, my wife and I were thrilled, of course, and the four of us had a big evening of celebration. But after the kids had gone home, a reaction set in. "Why, you're too young to be a grandfather," I said to myself. This was obviously untrue — I am 55. "Well, you don't *look* old enough," I said. This was even more ridiculous.

The truth is, the march of time is beyond our power to alter. So, accept and enjoy it.

2. DON'T LOSE YOUR COOL.

My wife has an infallible technique for spreading news. She telephones certain girl friends, pledges them to secrecy, then tells them the latest bulletin. Up to now the fastest-moving, hottest items have been surgical details. But I discovered that word of an impending grand-child is hotter still.

The very next afternoon I found myself the center of attention. My niece and several of her playmates (fractious ten-year-olds) spotted me half a block off and yelled in unison, "Hey, Grandpa!" Then they burst into giggles, jumping up and down and covering their mouths with their hands.

I had just escaped these moppets when the village cop drove slowly past, stuck his head out the patrol-car window, removed the cigar from his mouth and called, "Hey, Grandpa!"

Then that evening I found my wife looking at me with amusement and affection. She said gently, "Hey, Grandpa."

How can one keep his cool under these conditions? I have evolved a facial expression which I recommend to all men. When you're kidded, don't try to defend yourself; simply give an enigmatic smile that is ever so slightly touched with pride and modesty. Let them fig-ure *that* out....

3. GET YOURSELF A SPECIALTY. There will be competition in the family to handle and care for the baby and, frankly, there just

aren't enough jobs to go around. It is well for the grandfather to find some area where his services are unique. I chose photography. I reasoned that everyone would want a complete picture record of the child — asleep, awake, first smile, first tooth, first step. The "court photographer" becomes the indispensable man....

4. BE PATIENT WITH GRANDMA. Of all the adults involved, the one who will have the most difficulty adjusting to a new role will be Grandma, your wife. She is delighted to be a grandmother, but she wants it on her terms. During this period she is apt to say totally opposite things and not see any contradiction.

"Do you suppose they'll let us baby-sit much?" she said one evening. "No doubt *her* mother will see more of the baby than I will."

Minutes later she said, "I don't want them to get the idea that we're always available to baby-sit at their beck and call. I have my own life to live, too."

A grandfather must be careful not to agree (or disagree) with everything she says during this period. To find yourself stuck with one of her discarded positions can be a nerve-racking experience....

5. YOU ARE EXPECTED TO BOAST. Why not do so? You are *expected* to see your grand-child as the most beautiful and smartest baby ever born. Why try to be modest? For the first time in your life you are *expected* to indulge yourself. So don't knock the system.

That's all the time I have for advice — there's a car coming up the driveway bringing Jennifer for a visit. She knows me now and always greets me with a smile of incandescent radiance. Her parents and her grandmother claim it is the same smile she gives them, but I know the difference. Jennifer and I know the difference.

THE NEW JOYS IN HIS LIFE

In her article "Meet the New Sam Levenson — Grandfather," Helen Alpert describes the beloved American humorist's big new world of unceasing wonders — the world of grandparents.

"It's a revelation to me," he says. "Why didn't anybody tell me about this sooner? You get free laughs all day long."...

This time around, at sixty-three, Sam is ecstatic in his new role as grandfather. The birth of little Georgia two years ago suddenly swept him into a magical land of expanding new delights. Georgia is the daughter of his architect son Conrad and Conrad's wife Isabella. A few weeks ago a baby brother joined the family. "You know the old definitions of a genius? They're true! A genius is a stupid kid with grandparents. And you know the joke: 'Isn't it amazing how the dope who married your daughter could produce such a brilliant grandchild?'"

Laughingly he describes his lying on the floor playing with Georgia when she began pounding him with a hammer she discovered. What he lovingly called out, fending off the blows, was, "Look how nice she holds the hammer!"

Grandchildren are smarter than anybody. "But so," he adds, "are today's grandpas and grandmas...."

His lively new joys have also given him a new slant on mere mothers and fathers. "Those people are called Parents. Any kid who has been exposed to grandparents would never want to live with young, impatient, cranky parents. I often wonder why kids are obliged to leave home – why shouldn't the parents, instead, leave home? On the other hand," he says, "if we told our children the truth about the so-called joys of parenthood, they would never get married. So my wife Esther and I got a double-reward for hiding the truth...."

What has been called the "love affair" between the first and third generations has long been known to sociologists who still have never explored this "in depth" with barrels of statistics. A few years ago, one treatise pointed out a bit timidly that grandparents and grandchildren share a common enemy, the parents, against whom they must constantly plot in conspirators' glee. Grandfathers, grandmothers and grandchildren have never needed to be told this; they instinctively sense they have supporters and defenders in each other. "Grandma stands out as Public Defender Number One. Nobody in Washington or any world capitol can match her," is Sam's salute. "Remember how our own mother wanted to tear us from limb to limb at any provocation? Now it's the same woman who says sharply to her daughter, 'Don't you touch him. Reason with him. Did I ever hit you?' All the kid was doing was sawing a leg off the dining room table. Says Grandma: 'He's just playing.'

"There's no doubt that grandchildren are exceptionally smart. Did you ever see grandchildren stop you on the street or in a bus or on a plane to show you pictures of their grandparents and start bragging about them?"...

While Sam was finishing "In One Era & Out the Other," little Georgia was born. The book's final page is the letter he instantly wrote to her. "Georgia baby: We leave you a tradition with a future. The tender loving care of human beings will never become obsolete. People, even more than things, have to be restored, renewed, revived, reclaimed, and redeemed, and redeemed....Never throw out anybody.

"As you grow older you will discover that you have two hands. One for helping yourself, the other for helping others. While I was growing up I took as many hands as I gave. I still do.

"At our age we doubt whether we will make it to your wedding, but if you remember us on that day, we shall surely be there. Mazel tov...." He did not have to sign it: "Your Loving Grandfather and Thank You."

Set in Goudy Old Style,
a typeface designed by Frederic W. Goudy
and introduced in 1916.
Printed on Hallmark Eggshell Book paper.
Designed by Lilian Weytjens.